Dancing with the Morning Breeze

Dancing with the Morning Breeze

Poems that speak of light and shadows and of the people
in the dance of our lives.

by

Allegra Jostad Silberstein

Cover design by Shay Culligan
Cover image by Daniel Sessler

ISBN: 978-1-63980-166-4

Kelsay Books
502 South 1040 East, A-119
American Fork, Utah 84003
Kelsaybooks.com

Acknowledgments

I am grateful to the following publications where these poems first appeared, some in a slightly altered form.

California Quarterly: "When I Met My Muse," "Let it Be," "Catch the Heart Off-Guard," "Blessings"
Dad's Desk: "Camel Rock"
Last Leaves: "The Mask of Stillness"
Munyori Literary Journal: "I leave the loneliness of words"
Orchards Poetry Journal: "The Deepening Pool"
Poetry Pacific: "Quantum Entanglement"
Proverse Anthology: "Encounter," "Bending into Blue"
Sacramento Voices: "We Hold On" (title was "In a Loose Pocket")
Song of the San Joaquin: "My Father's Shoes," "Bringing in a Song," "Winnowing," "Opening"
Tule Review: "A Room of One's Own"
WTF #19: "Into the Cluttered Dark"

* "Circles of Light" was the grand prize winner in the 2018 Dancing Poetry Contest.

Contents

I Listen

to the quiet song of breath
the words riding on air
place them tenderly on the page.

Love is a firefly
flickering in dark chambers
of the heart.

You are in the everywhere
where I search
lost in long shadows.

I want to go to sleep with you
your body close to mine
sing my song for you.

The sun leaves a mystery
of blush in the hush
of a parting day.

Into the Forest

after a painting by Edvard Munch

We move through blue threads
that cut across our lives

into the forest
into the shadow lands

where a bit of blue shines
through the tops of Norway Pines

and in a purple mist
the yellow bird sings.

Our feet tread upward
in a land all mountains and valleys

your arm around me
mine around you

our heads lean
one onto the other.

We know not where we go
nor even the place we seek.

The compass of our heart
leads the way.

Between blue threads
a yellow bird sings.

Infinite Holdings

Loss comes
The world shakes
Something within holds
A mourning dove awakes.

Beauty of bare branches
Swelling buds parting—
The touch of sunlight
In the distance a dog barks.

When you find peace
Everything falls into place
Don't wait
You can't stop the world's race.

Tattoo of blossoms
Beauty the goal
Beads, rings and painted things
Infinite soul.

This is a Chinese form invented by Dr. Fan Kuanling called Hsinku. It has 4 lines and the 2nd and 4th rhyme. The first 3 lines set up a situation, and the 4th gives an unexpected or unique ending.

The Ebb and Flow

Returning tides
speak to me
bring understanding
that carries me out
of a place of fear

and your kiss
so clear I learn . . .

knowing
we are made of water
force and innocence
flowing
from this to that.

Bending into Blue

Caught in cabin-dreams
I rest my head
in branches of living green

in a mystery of blue
in the miracle of morning
that lights windows
where I slept
where dreams entered
unannounced

waking, I put aside
unborn issues
lurking in secret places
and rise to meet this day

questing—in meditation—
beneath the valley oak
with branches that hover like
wings of my better angel
held in dawn-light

with living movement
between the leaves—
a green singing
calls my name.

Camel Rock

I never thought to seek my muse
such elegance and special care
foreign to the rock-rimmed farm
that shaded my young years

but I remember long walks
across the ridge to an outcropping
of weathered limestone
we called Camel Rock

remember climbing
to sit astride
and the ride there
to distances . . .

Into the cluttered dark

I have breached infinity, you tell me . . .
as if broken through

as if a promise has not been kept,
or a whale has breached the water.

The waves break on our ship—
white horses stampede there.

Spirit in the never-ending
seeks a voice in the now.

Heather sprouts its way through
a crack in the cliff.

You peek through the knotholes
on a wooden fence.

Someone calls on God
to bring rain . . . to bring death.

Ghosts tender the mind
recalling rant.

So loud, the ticking of a wall clock,
the foundation must tremble.

A white bear plods into the night
breaking through the crusted snow.

I leave the loneliness of words

~~into night~~
a solace of stars.

Looking up
something inside widens.

Breath expands
into space unfathomed.

I am spell caught
in the high call of an owl

for a few moments
held in an unfathered universe.

Bringing in a Song

Beneath the quiet
of a cloudy day
a sparrow is singing.

Pine trees pointing
reach beyond this dark quiet
toward light.

In this time of isolation
we're not alone completely
for somewhere there is singing.

My tall clock talks . . . but
the rhythm of its tick and tock
does not disturb my quiet.

At the edge of thought
in a dizzy half-dream place
I sing with the dreamers.

Beyond the clouds
there is sunlight of song,
beneath the quiet of sunset
a sparrow sings.

Let it be

Let yourself be silently drawn
by the stronger pull of what you love
                                        —Rumi

Dive into the unknown and let
it be in the country of yourself
however uncomfortable that may be.

Enter this mystery turning silently
as if in a ritual dance
drawn by gravitation and levitation,

altered by breath into spaces
between vertebrae, the ribs and belly
into knowledge stronger

than the mind-ordered pull
that keeps telling over and over
of should and should not,

dismaying what
the heart's beating tells you—
whispering softly of love.

Seeing into Darkness

Seeing into darkness is clarity—
this is called practicing for eternity
                              —Lao-tzu

I close my eyes to practice
seeing into darkness.
The knowledge of breath
felt but unseen
a promise of eternity.

Wind sings in my veins.
With a song there
I do not fear the dark.

With open eyes
I see the bare vines
on my grape arbor
and signs of swelling buds.

Morning light streaming
through the pines
edges them with gold
like some ancient book of wisdom.

A small wooden box waits
to hold my ashes
when this body of mine is gone.

A Room of One's Own

thanks to Virginia Woolf for the title

I ought to be writing learned poems, their wisdom gleaming starkly as Georgia O'Keeffe's clean picked bones against yellow desert sands. (How long have I got to make my mark in this world?) Instead, I sit with Grandfather at the hospital . . . caress his hands, mottled dark with injuries from falls, skin slack and strangely soft, incongruous black hairs growing young and strong between knuckles that stretch out of his skin like mountain peaks. His beard and little halo of hair, all salty silver with pepper touch, gives him a saintly look.

I try to talk. It's hard. With his one hearing aid lost and the other not working well, what he hears is me speaking nonsense. He repeats what he has heard, checking for accuracy (he always did), wondering, I suppose, if my mind were weakening. I speak again, slower, enunciating each word until we come to some compromise of meaning. (I should apply for a job negotiating treaties with the hard-of-hearing leaders of this world.)

Occasionally, there's a flash of old wit and his eye twinkles. He has only one. Out of the blue, remembering perhaps some bit of a play or poem he asks me . . . *Irish eyes or English eyes.* I smile and answer, *Both* going with the tide rather than striving for some stable base of comprehension.

I hold his hand. He holds onto mirages, sure that a certain young nurse wants to get into his bed. Restless in his wheelchair, he looks toward the door of his hospital room and speaks with longing; *if I could just get through, I could find my room* . . .

He speaks for me, too. I want to find my place: that *Room of One's Own* . . . if I could just get through.

The Mask of Stillness

Nothing is the solace for
    what's the matter now

    Deep footprints
drag their shadows behind them

        There is stillness between
in the rhythm of tick and tock

Paper from pulp of the felled tree
    longs for the flow of words

    Haystacks do not grieve
      the lost needle

    Dark paragraphs
dangle new prophets before us

    Stillness in the mountains
      awaits the unmasking

Invitations

Morning colors the horizon
but has not chased away the moon:
this white moth in the far sky
sends notes from the night.

Open window, fluttering curtain
the quiet of breath
that flows into soul where
angels enter willingly.

Beyond the bare branches
of the walnut trees
singing pines sway—
dance with the morning breeze.

Catch the Heart Off-Guard

a line from Seamus Heaney

In your body I heard rivers
sing their way to the ocean,
your heartbeat the pounding surf.

You came unannounced
out of the night's dream
like morning dew.

Now the wind shouts your name,
you are the reason
of my evening song.

Stars of the night
shine in your eyes
and I—alive in your dream

am kissed
by the mouth of a breeze.
A nightingale sings to the moon.

Of Canaries and Peonies

inspired by Hokusai painting: Canary and Peony

My uncle was a canary
caged by his farm.
He loved to play the piano.

My uncle planted peonies
to blossom in his cage
and tulips to welcome spring.

He tended to his cows
to the tilling of the land
but his flowers mattered most . . .

he always was in need
and we his hilltop neighbor
helped to gather in the hay

to feed his cows in the long winter.
Though our barn was full, we had no
peonies to blossom in the spring.

A canary curves
its flight into the waiting
flower-songs of May.

My Father's Shoes

after Van Gogh's painting of a pair of shoes

Van Gogh found the beauty
of a pair of worn shoes
laces undone
the day's work finished
marked by signs
of wear and tear of daily use.
They stand sanctified
in a pool of golden light.

I remember my father's shoes
returned to kitchen light and warmth
after he cared for the cattle
bedding them for the night.
Van Gogh enlightens me
to beauty I did not appreciate
in those long ago years—
my father's worn shoes.

In a Drift of Spirit

for Elizabeth

When my sister goes to bed
she puts a pillow by her side
then turns away to sleep.

She feels the warmth
the comfort at her back
like love nearby . . .

imagination carries
her in a drift of spirit
easing distances . . .

here with her husband
through laughter and tears
she has slept for sixty years.

When my sister rises
she puts the pillow aside
abiding in the new day's presence.

Blessings

a blade of grass still holding pearls of morning rain,
a broken branch: redwood tree delights my nose
narcissus blossoming all along the fence
one daffodil in the middle of the orchard
swollen buds bursting into white on the almond trees
green leaves sprouting on the elderberry:
blessings counted this day . . .

and may the blessing of rain be for you
when you have a raincoat and umbrella,
the blessing of sunlight be for you
when you have sunglasses and a wide brimmed hat,
the blessing of tears be for you when joy flows so swiftly
through your body it cannot be contained
the blessing of touch be for you when strictures
cannot bind the rush of living water

these, too, be blessings:
a piece of glass honed by the sea
into an amber heart
an empty bottle that held perfume
two grapefruit clinging to the same twig
a piece of petrified wood with little holes
where worms lived
a poem known by heart

Where Did Lilacs Go

April came
raw and biting
breeding lilacs
out of the dead land

    where, Eliot,
    where did lilacs go

only withered fronds remain
fragrance gone
remembered aroma
haunts autumn days

riots of color
do not obliterate—
memory's curve
harks back

beneath my feet
the crusted ground
and little dust clouds—
until the rain comes

pounding upon us
piercing the hardened soil
where dream seeds sprout
in rain drenched earth

    here, Eliot,
    here in this living earth

the strong root
waits through the cold winter
and lilacs blossom
when April comes again.

Winnowing

trees light a new day
sun-gold
tangled in branches

    does this soft breeze
       bring words
    riding on your breath . . .

a hunger of blossoming
awaits
the honeyed visit of the bees

    have you heard the grass
       laughing
    with the snapping wind . . .

inlets of song-sound
flow
into deeper ground

    can one turn the page
       from first line
    to the last litany of loss . . .

in the turn of my mind
a small space
searches for landings

Autumn

Touch me
let me know I am alive

in this holy place we walk
this moment of autumn light

this gold and orange blaze
of aspen trees

memory quivers like trees
in water mirrored layers

in this stream
soul could be one kiss

Touch me
let me know I am alive

Quantum Entanglement

When I first heard these words
first heard the vague explanation
of particles entangled
I thought to myself, of course,
the heart knew it all along:
the enchanted evening syndrome
where you see someone across the
crowded room and know you're
connected . . .

> *I've found out*
> *there's a whole branch of physics*
> *dealing with all the properties*
> *and applications of photons*
> *as a means of transmitting*
> *information*
>
> *scientists use a laser-beam...*
> *fire it through a type of crystal*
> *and cause individual photons*
> *to be split into pairs:*
> *entangled photons that*
> *can communicate even though*
> *separated by long*
> *distances.*

We have evolved
through years and centuries . . .
who knows what split particles
have entered . . . who knows
the unknown
        quantum entanglements
that teach
        the strumming of the heart

Encounter

Across the table our eyes tied
in a speck of time as if by some ancient cord
your dark eyes released for a moment
from the words you were reading . . .
mine giving reply.

Old or young, we're not immune
to a certain look that opens us
that moves through an inner wall
like seepage between layered limestone
in a northern springtime.

You held me in your eyes
—almost that is enough—
though yearning thighs ache for more . . .
I long to break commandments
to fly, to swim into surprise.

You are too old an inner voice chides
your face has wrinkles
even though your eyes hold light
the years tell their stories
no matter what the heart decries.

Perhaps this touch was second sight
crossing a great divide: a time warp—
a table's width eclipsing years
to a time we loved one another—
I ride the long shadows.

Circles of Light

Moon-woman cuts a circle of light
in the misty sky with a golden glow
hiding what lies behind & beyond—
flames of desire we cannot know.

In the misty sky a golden glow
a longing perhaps for hidden stars
—flames of desire within us grow—
darkling dreams catch us unaware.

Longings for something hidden
in cocoons for woven silk
and darkling dreams catch us—
Moon-woman's magic distilled.

Soft to touch as woven silk
lovers encircled by night.
In the misty sky a golden glow.
Moon-woman cuts a circle of light.

Opening

I would travel into time's delight
with songs of larks to tell their tales to me
that bring again the peace of field and tree
and stay the shadows of the coming night.

And when I've stumbled into second sight
there'll be a sacred place that sets me free
for all the things that I was meant to be
where I once feared to go but now I might.

Insistent as the ticking of the clock
inviting as the tunes that make me dance
quiet as the clouds in their display
I hear a whisper in a roadside rock
and feel it bidding me to take a chance
to open gates I thought had blocked my way.

When I met my muse

my almost true story in response to William Stafford's meeting of his muse

When I met my muse on my little acre
I just glanced at her and then moved on
without a thought
for muses come and muses go
but weeds hold out for many a day.

Her voice then belted out to me
in tones I could not ignore . . .
I don't give a fig
for foxtails or Bermuda grass
and I've sent my friend, the fox,
to startle you and bring you to your senses.

A vain threat I thought,
but then I saw a fox, walking
on the trunk of a fallen over pine tree
like a bridge to heaven knows where
—she saw me and

ran away—
just like a muse, I thought.
A second-thought came,
as they often do . . .

though foxtails are a common sight
any hour of the day
a tail upon a real fox is something
I need to write about
in my book of everyday poems.
—My muse must be amused.

In Our Sweet Ruin

We are drawn into the moon
the aching place of no return—
the parting time that comes too soon

This precious time together
that circles round as we turn
drawn into the moon.

Your hand in mine
feeds all that in me yearns
to forget the parting that comes too soon.

Be it midnight or morning
the sun, its reflection or here, burns
we're drawn into the moon.

That we are old in our sweet ruin
is of no concern
for the parting time is coming soon.

Your hand holding mine
shelters as if a promise of return…
as we are drawn into the moon
the parting time that comes too soon.

The Deepening Pool

I am in need of peace that will flow
over my body's waiting parts, my lips
my face, my limbs, even my fingertips,
in arching time with breathing deep and slow:
the breath for letting inner tensions go
the breath that lets our spirits move ahead
that leaves behind all thoughts of fear and dread
and brings instead a gift of sunset glow

a twilight time that's like a melody
softly played, unwinding like a spool
holding thread that mends a quilt for the deep
quiet of the coming night when all we need
is the essence of the deepening pool
the easy rhythm of our healing sleep.

In the long shadow

sing into the jade song
the fallen tree
the winged floating
gentle in the night-shade air
where juniper thrusts its needles

walk into carnelian space
the autumn forest
bird song and falling leaves
wait in this wood temple
a full moon makes long shadows

return into lapis lazuli: the healing
the breath
the blue humming
in time before time
where the self becomes aware

The Strong Pull

Tonight, under a full moon
all things seem possible and soon
my thoughts revel in dark magic
sweeter than honey—a gladsome trick.

I breathe the universe into my soul
feeling within infinite and whole
each atom of mine entwined
somehow, in the cosmic mind . . .

moon and stars in a cloudless sky
unreasoning reasons do not explain why
their light empowers a flight
bringing you here, bedded in night.

I breathe you into my heart,
where no rules will keep us apart.

We Hold On

Twilight is a lamp
neither sold nor bought.

After the burning
the returning storms.

In the unwinding
a dark mapping of the land.

We hold on to small change
in a loose pocket.

If I Forget

If I forget what day it is
and what I meant to do
remind me that I loved to swing.

If I forget where I put my keys
and what I came here for
remind me of ripening blackberries.

If I forget the hour we were to meet
or the name of a friend
remind me with the scent of clover.

If I forget to tie my shoes
and stumble into night
remind me as the stars begin to sing.

About the Author

Allegra Jostad Silberstein grew up on a farm in Wisconsin but has lived in California since 1963. Her love of poetry began as a child . . . her mother would recite poems as she worked. In addition to three chapbooks of poetry, she has been widely published in journals, with a growing number online. Her first book of poems, *West of Angels, was* published by Cold River Press in March of 2015. In March of 2010, she became the first Poet Laureate for the city of Davis, California, serving for two years. She also dances with the Third Stage dance company and sings with Threshold Choir.